T0193182

codes of change
take shape

11

iUniverse, Inc.
Bloomington

codes of change
take shape

iUniverse books may be ordered through booksellers or by contacting:

iUniverse
1663 Liberty Drive
Bloomington, IN 47403
www.iuniverse.com
1-800-Authors (1-800-288-4677)

ISBN: 978-1-4697-8059-7 (sc)
ISBN: 978-1-4697-8058-0 (e)

Printed in the United States of America

iUniverse rev. date: 2/22/2012

codes of change

take shape

11

page 1

page 64

book 1 things thought between worlds 11

book 2 indigo 7 i am 11

book 3 codes of change take shape 11

first flow

namaste

intuition
intellect
balance

will
flow
allow
love

yes sometimes it's nice 2 end
songs in the middle assuming
the next 1 resumes the ending

1112234455566788999
NUMBERS 5 LETTERS
STRUCTURE
SYNTAX
5 4 3 2
1

be 3 effect 2 cause 1 effect 1

when i'm standing and i recognize 1 insight
waiting 4 writing 3 often 1 forgets 5
at least i know i learned it 1 time
now i know 2 write 1 2 5

on my bicycle under a tree
cars pass me by 1
do they notice
3

so sound it out as each word makes sound
yes i'll read it as provided yes i'll sound it
5 1 may not know when but yes comes 5
allow 4 5 adjustment 1 commencement

begun

likewise
patience stay wise
assisting change
presenting
antroaaaaa

aaaajraaaaaaaraaaaa
akraaroaraaa

WWWWWWWOOOooooooook
a
ak
aKkaaaaaaaaakaaaaaaaaawaaaaaaaaw

aWawaaacf
aWcaW
OacaO
WaOC
c
aWca
wckakaKcAWDOD
{ifo
qf{_
aaaaaaaaaAA

S
SS
SOME HELICOPTER JUST FLEW BYHa
AAwawawaaa
iAIAAAAAAAIA
I
aw
ijJDDWDA

done so much
waited long
enough

0 acceptance
1 recognition (or no)
2 yes
3 divine
4 change
5 acknowledgment of change
6 assistance
7 creativity ~ creator
8 consciousness ~ masculine
9 nature ~ feminine
knowledge
communication
conversation
input
output
registration

1
i know i'm weird and so are you
LOOK
this weird took us this long to get 2
so love the weird that is
at peace to remain
weird yet true
regardless 3
2

~

wise 1 told 3 life was lived 4 dying
true 2 blossoms wilt 1 time 5
1 3 blossom as the moment
as the wilting is 3 ending
4

~

5
pleasing he
charming she
before he knew she saw him
leave
6

~

7
namaste
8

a coiled snake before a well
motives unclear
darkness surrounds
thus THIS 1 stares
remembering the nightmare
void of THAT fear
curious
understanding
my first memory SAW fear
brilliant
nightmare
my first memory
now HERE

clock tock
22:55
the face of the mirror present
reflecting amplified intentions
14
now 4 review
as 3 mirror 5 being
assist THIS thinking presently
22:56
moment complete
life before sense 5 intention
focused thoughts manifest
6
23:22
assistance
4 2 1 will allow 3
link 2 3 greater entirety
1111
presence
assistance
23:33
1
all 1 must do 5
accept 1
yes 2
accept 3
yes i 4
blink twice i
think yes
5

creativity exercises
see BE room 2 SEE
destroyed by 1 storm
renewed 5 sound

work

notice SEE visualize
passing wind patterns 3
evaporation
condensation
now appreciate now

rest

make goal
give shape
watch change
3 feel 2 manifesting

1

marble rolling away
throughout mindscape
marble STAY before 1
follow marble 2 imagination

play

fire
change as seen 5 variability
essence 2 3 ongoing miracle
allowing beginning 2 new
cyclical
time 4 being
catalyst 4 changes
past present fire future
burn fire burning brighter
animated force seen 3 destroying
fire
burning with THIS light
all the fear the flame INSIDE
with this white light absorb INSIGHT
fire is as is fire
ash
fire renew fire welcome
cyclical fires naturally burning
life 4 fire breath technique
beginning 2 change
seed 4 new
mind make fire 1
man water fire
sm0ke

just so beautiful
light shone through water
magnificence
twinkle of light from another's eye
inducing the change
ALLOW
all is change
FEEL
as the change
yet unconcerned
BE
the change
AS IT IS
light reflects
BE
FREE
twinkling eye
accepting
CHANGE
remain
stay
accepted
gained

literal release
under trees leaves fall embracing 3 breeze
regardless what we do know START 2
leaves flow breeze acceptance understanding
4 LOVE 4
leaves from trees like nerves from the ground
reaching up and out around 1 conscious cell
the earth 1 planet
providing the elements
not pollution
nor greed
yet cut
FALL
trees
4 all they do is grow 1
SAW
leaves
falling
sound
crashing
planetary stability endangered
thanks 2 3
the 1 2 change
namaste

ninja
walk on surfaces quietly
now add speed
silently
learn use tools
swiftly change
the rules
the mask
the pass
stop
return when clear
stay
night is day
say
this the way
change
take away
wait
the blade
BELAY
the chosen form now settle score
path the pave 4 silent change
stay unseen stay
silently

not sure why this list is weird but
smile showing too much teeth
laughter
small talk
with a capital letter
first
because it was already there
1 going last
not having
grass
the sedentary
people
not allowing
change
with concern
who blame
shame

not sure why part 2
judging
me
4
fun
not staying with the popular 1
so be as this or else
some sort of block
if it's not done this way
repercussions
your way
laughing
shaking hands
writing haha
without laughing
because 1 won't
the rubik's cube
paradox
an end to this
magic trick
measures of intelligence
BEING UNAWARE 2 1 ANSWER
is this a belly button or a navel
TOMATO OR TOMATO
hAHa

not sure why part 3
following someone
it just feels right
lovely taboo
laughing out loud
and i now pronounce you
LOL
i know right
music capturing
subtle sense
solid
that's that slang
stay off my bed
dog is what i call my people
people putting clothes on animals
animals outsmarting humans
straight up real talk
something better than
current technology
why size 33 is so hard to find
things varying
depending on
companies
how i just know
what 2 say
next

oh
i forgot 2 REMEMBER.
yes OF COURSE.
i should.
it makes sense.
i'll be sure 2 mention
ok so
the creak in the wall told me to tell you
number
2
ok i did it.
i should have wrote this earlier
ok should i stop now?
the air conditioning turned on…
i forgot to breathe but didn't notice until…
2 clicks from the wall
BREATHE
click
1
i must sound so-
-click-
.

always maintain discipline
everyone is crazy
11.

playing instead of learning
on some level
recognize the waiting
i see nothing
modest 3
as I am
i proceed
in the present
state of mind
recognize THE need
2
want what WISDOM wills within
4
show 3 something
3 love learning
4
this compilations of exertions
1
the more i write
the more i can write
the more i can express what it is that i 5
the more i can write 4 1 extended time
i have no clue what's after this
this comes after that does finish
1 at a time XI
all things in time 2 SMILE

realizations are fun
1
gaining balance
with no arms
flow like snake do
left right before move
nothing slow motion
2
children wiser than we
3
the source of what's SO funny
4
I
am ever
5
inside
6
heel raised toes planted foot angled
hi 7
come ally
8
HE
fInd
SHE
9
RETURNing

remove the clocks
now stay
set an alarm 4 when 2 needs 1
stay
present tense
ok
it's easy
ENTRAIN
appreciate the sun
change 4 time is set 5 sun
synchronize life 2 5 moon
the moon FEEL more pull than the TIME clock
synchronicity increasing naturally
3

ribbons of light originate inside
though eyes can
pathways 4 energy expand
as i change
inside i
always growing
3
i am i can i will BE free
something simple someone sees
inside day is night the latent day
latent salient SALIENT stay
now yes understand
yes now
ok
light 1 forming
close 2 eyes
third eye
RISE
3

secret HOLDING strangers
inside acquaintances
1 see 5 mirrors
check 4 5 progress
1 2 acknowledge presence
5 smiling
BREATHing
when i
think so
they 2 know
who
but they won't say
lovingly
the strangeR
WAY

sightless lovers
enter 3 warm feeling surrounding
where are you ? here my love
let me share
i do hear you set me free
what be this can i not see ? yes need not see this
now form still sight absent
sightless i 3 seen as free
sightless lovers adrift 5 sea

synchronicity
experiential fractal sequencing
tesseract logically functioning
foresight define growing
construct symmetry
opportunity
structure
déjà vu
allow
2
procession
delta theta alpha beta 3 5 gamma
connection 4 inside
waking
free will link
unrecognized
a coincidence
recognize 5 synchronicity
~
courtesy of feminine wise
draw an 8 on paper with INTENT in mind
this intent is now your 4 WISH 4
8 days 8 carrying 8 in your presence
AT 11:11 sun up sun down 2 find 1 mirror 0
focused on reflected 8 affirming wish 8 times 8
MINIMUM energetic requirements
30 seconds moonlight and 2 minutes if cloudy
every night
3
on the 8th night after 11:11pm
burn the 8
be receptive as always stay open

that random chest pain
knives affect breathing
inhale stop breath here
exhale hurt chest there
wait
all 1 can
2
reflect
3
the other day i learned something
involving accepting color green
what if i don't listen
interrupting as if disciplining
1
the first time i felt the knives and knew why
no doubt i deserved that
1
knife
5
painful reminder
this time was brief
4
1
knife
monitor thoughts 5 strike
watershed
2
1
knife

the beast caught walking
stare at this thing distracting
showing teeth should this see 3
leave before unfavorably ending
and peace befell the beast
while walking

yes
all 2 need
.
.
all
2
3
.
.
.
.
.
.
.
.
.
.

YES

●

●

second flow

when shadows outreach bodies IDEAL outdoors
sunlight energy 1 safely absorbing

presence correlates creativity

acceptance

3

1 answer
i would ask
what was before me
yes 5 cease 4 me 2 be
imagine I continue 3

why do i chew my lips?
you are not at peace.
how do i find peace?
stop chewing your lips.

beast with pens
if i don't reason
yet i do listen
staying centered
with a pen intending writing
something unconcerning happens

the best laxative
emotional clearing
pass this test
wake the rest
clear the mess
now watch
this
wonderfully
relieving

2

look 3 face
openings 4 sensing
remove 1 sense
what 2 looking

falling leaves arrange 2 show 3 I
Ching i possess 2 n0t obsess
consult when NEEDing 6
CURIOUSITY explained
this is what
is looks at
CHANGE

transcend tense when ready 2 begin
*

stay centered and process change
now 1 same has change 2 stay
*

relating coordinates 1 functional lesson
abilities increase 2 strengthening 1 breathe 3
something tells when this 1 ending
*

light code entropy
stealth transmission
liberat
ing

yes ___
not the keeper of ___
choose or be left ___
right not wrong when ___
as 2 wish 2 stop ___
knowledge ___ helps choose
signaling ___ happening
2
yes ___ is ___ yes
___ is what IS needed ___ grow
replace ___ with 2 if ___ is you
take no offense 2 test the rule
especially when the rule tests

___

intimidation 4 novice 1
unaccepted 5 experience
fearing change 1 conditioning
before 3 accepting novelty
fear lesson 2 be learned
acceptance 4 normal
let it be
lest
scary DISTRACT away
unknown 5 until
allowed
inside

motivational speech
2
encourage motion
insisting 3 notion
you recognize you
inside
what moves you
irony being
people motivating people
as if motivation was previously unavailable
1

into the zone where is shields this
stay with text 2 get through yes
knowledge secret with 1 veil
veil stay hid inside 5 mind
peer beyond 2 know 4 i
1 2 forget 3 mind 5 I
breathe
the more i not the more i learn
not is done when time is mind
being greater without need
presence comprehension
feel acceptance enter
ing

on my 2.1 speaker stereo 1 day a speaker broke
on my extra bass earbud headphones 1 right ear
stop
i removed the speaker and the earbud from each
set
up
like there is some weird type benefit from listening
1
left
ear
2
sounding proper
2
curiously affecting music
music from 1 speaker 3
2 creates a ripple wave
the curious way
the CHANGING
ri66le
wave

now i am monster
monster stay changing
not always wanted
I direct needs 3
reflection of
wisdom
guised i am
hidden
save for the need
3
change not observed
needs be

~

beauty becoming
lesser transmuting
amusing learning
hidden behind
being unfolding
layers connected
body united
despite 1 layer seen as
present
i 3 greatness underneath
i delight the i that sees
deep enough i presenting
all the way i cannot see
need only see 3
enough
4
3

i hear patterns unlocking
growth uninterrupted
i flow i know i stop
pattern encoded
change reflecting
as 1 message
sharing light
3
inside laughter
4 unblocking pathways i
would and could thus i 2
5
what
without i
night change day night restore
light
meaning transcend language
BARRIER

~

affirming
while burning
5 ritual lighting
2 strengthen intention
whilst it's on fire

set the fire
sight burns bright
4 resonant light
fire transform ladder
5
start 2 climb 1 ascend i
chamber password
i2enter
lighter2i5
WHY 2 NEED RECEIVE
understanding
PRESENTing
~
ok then
find a perch 2 stay up there
see the body extended as needed
take shape needed 4 touching ground
strength lives inside wise exercise 5
sit
extend 4 room
expand 2 mind
now let 5 your normal 2
2 is 1 expansive 2
3 presents 4
awareness
improves
5

this thing inside my head is bright
it's focused inward opened light
shining past cathedral bridges
there this is
1 transmitting receiver 3
recently relocated i
i find it down right amazing i
know this excitement will pass with time
all i can say 4 now is
i
open now hole in
1

~

more on the receiver
i focus inside head open inward i
pass what forms pass 4 imagination 4
dark and light present inner sight
gold and blue mixing other colors 2
mineral rainbows shading constellations
i sink say might me unfocused thoughts
3

i spent some time writing things i would
about me yet simultaneously 4 love
i set them on fire every half hour
until i felt i finished
i
wrote 4 changing 5 life
what is written and burned 2 become 3
attractive technique
awareness 4 karma
always lovingly
purposefully
1

~

1 day i wrote words and numbers
i set them on fire every half hour
most 5 focus 1 being 4 love
prosperity 2 happiness
changing 5 reality
yes
my devotion made
magic 4 3 and soon i did see
what eventuates in time 1 mind
intent interacting 5 attraction 2 i
WILL 2 love in all these forms 5
set on fire 2 be
realized

3 always loves 2
when you're gone you're still around
synchronized lives 5 links 2 minds
love bonds all 2 breathe 4 3
life pattern 4 presenting 3
knowing 2 always love
us
feeling
as 2 is
change assists
how we
live
changing again
feeling synchronized with 3
unconcerned 2 adjust
BREATHE
~
the story of the triggered rainbow
2 relive the sight see light
1 begins 2 make light grow
faster radiating force
color which happens
first is last
now 2
third eye extrasensory light
withstand coloring
bathe in light
energizing
5
1 light source vibrating before 3
spark light fractal pattern begin
emerge 2 fill space horizon
trigger rainbow container
rainbow recharge 1222
rainbow recharge 2

here is what i did
i was alone in sunlight with music
placing my hands before me i slowed
rhythm
movement made 1 ball 2 energy
i felt its presence
and when it was
ready
i raised it to the sky
ball 2 rise absorb sunlight
then i returned it 2 5 body

~

how 2 create 1 energy ball
hands visualizing apart
palms coming together
slowly bring closer
when 2 feel
resistance
expand allow grow
slowly bring in palms
expand but not too fast
help it let it feel its presence

~

how 2 prepare 4
well lit outdoor location
walk in a circle
stand in the middle
this is 5 circle
burn intention papers 0 1 2
ash in the center
wind blows and rain cleans
bodily essence activates
3
this circle is an extension of
3

3 times in 3 days i closed my eyes 2 3
something insisting i not 2 see
1 time i
heard a beautifully complex song
1 time i
synced my breathing 2 swallow something
1 time i
learned regarding sexuality
always i
interacted energetically 3 obey all instructions
third eye energy body transformation 5
sensation rippling 4 benefiting
i
keep eyes closed
feeling different
eyes stay closed
this is change
must obey
left eye right eye
now deep breath
sigh
then i knew why
this
was

2

third flow

this literal canvas recant 4 5 madness

resume everyday new

masculine
feminine
left balance right

when i ACKNOWLEDGEd an animal
quiet respect 2 calm breath speed
falling leaf 3 message received
BREEZE acknowledging LEAVE

loving monster want FIND partner
good CHOICE LUCK CHOSE 1 lucky monster

1 person 2 bicycle 3 fly down on purpose 4 why else i love the breeze

stranger 5 support
2 meet 3
would 2 like 2 confide 5 3
2 would grow 3 would leave
benefit
changing
karma
3

as i STOP i forget 2 need 2 blink
before 1 OBJECT intersects SEE
3 blink twice then 2 cross
3

claiming it's a rise but all 1 sees is
5

nay process processed foods laugh
i know i can but why do that
add that to the vegan rhyme
now i eat most raw food diet

to be considered for a moment
if you think you got it PROCEED
it's the same as if you didn't RECEIVE

it's nice being able to do stuff
whatever that stuff may be
it's all good with me
i'm just glad to do it
do what you need
i won't stop you
i actually love it
always chilling
tranquil dark
handling it
eventually
arranged
intuitive
intellect
respect
word

perception is changing
awareness is perception
acceptance changes awareness

eat the entire fruit
save the stem
eat all seeds
unless
1

3

experience yields
knowledge exchange
2
life 1 progress 4 wisdom 5 mind
I

kundalini awakening
as i
3
when it comes 1 must stay calm 4 2 happening 1
now wait
get comfortable
in time it comes
now
inhale i know this ride i appreciate sigh
overwhelmingWITHpresentsMIGHT
ok stop leave now lay down NOW
laying on my back alone
free of judgment
like orgasms
intimate
moment 2
automatically
accommodating
subtle fluctuations
vigilance 1 begins surging
eyes light up 2 end up closed
i think my back might scream HAVE FAITH
easy why 1 might think STOP
kundalini kundalini
energizing
curiously
feeling
differently
up and down
separation thins
something changes 3
hearing sound inside body
i swear i hear my spinal column
sound 1 seashell 2 make 1 hear noise
inside
change
expands
it travels upward resting everywhere
intense insight withstand this might

i cannot watch most sex videos
absence involved 2 need 2 sync
love wisdom 4 couples 2 in sync
when 2 minds 1 time 3 learn
many functions 4 1 sex life
climax review conclusion
ingesting 5 promptly i
remember my spine
energy increases
beginning
WITH
4
overwhelmed WITH
these flowing rivers beneath my skin
this is my body but this thing is not me
all veins pulsing it won't stop breathing not me
5
i start moving backward attempting 2 escape 3
has it always been like this i don't think i can return
CHANGE
changed 1 full circle
2
stop
3
normal
now return
1
2
3
yes change leaves
3
returned normalcy
i know i changed but now i'm cool
i love my body
my spine feels fine
i am
5
lover of life

is it ok to not believe in change

wise minds change 5 life reflects gain
ok good now come around again
welcome wisdom within
again
ok
1
thankfully positively absolutely masterfully
…
it is not about the master choosing path
..
i feel so young i must think old
….
before war wife come back soon
this will not
ok
again
apprentice achieving perpetual motion
……
astrology sign your rise
…
rest period over
…..
i resolve new send the 2 in
..
i blink 2 be understood 3
take away the 3
ok
ok
the challenge is writing it as 2 say
as they'll read it as 5 speaks sounds
2 for 1
..
when 1 in sync find mind synchronicity time
..
changing task 4 exercise completed
.
has been unknown 4 such a long time 5

now we're waking up 2 mind
this 2 means 4 we 5 appreciate I
loving waking 2 1 life
5
we know they say we only use a small percent
well those numbers are 2 change
2 goes on forever 2
1

~

come and get some wood my tree has fallen

~

weird is as weird does things smart likes
hello i
i will work on how i greet 3
2
i need some help with things troubling 3
Namaste
well i'm tired of the same so when will 2 change
momentarily
well i'm waiting waiting 2 anxiously patient
known
ready
4
lightworkers unite with the passage of time
5
facebook profile werdna backward
11
friend request accepted
1

you'll just have to wait this ride out
as long as you're present love reigns
if your eyes were 2 open 2 become the sky
here you are before 1 tree of life
hold your eye open 2 the moment
see life shift acknowledging change
will intend this on 1 paper 2 burn later ON
loud sight drift light
yes 2 loves 3
the closer 2 ride will rise up silent force called mighty
life
3
3 blinks 2 times
follow this within the realm of the tree 4 the call
this tree 3 began
in the
fall
déjà vu schedule 2 see time flow 5 ways 4 shows
coincide yes 2 no mind balance gender aspect 5
the reason this continues is 4 i love the feeling
when i get it right it's like i get a dose
life

JOURNEY 2 CONSCIOUSNESS
ok consciousness
that's what's up
yes you agree
i'll take it from here
as you will
continue seeing your life positively speed
a good start
appreciate
Namaste
word
1
burning this book beneficial 2 3
1
derisleep waken
that's pretty neat
that's what was thought
take a nap asap it's not a typo
settling in amidst mist changes
nicely put 2 love never loses sight
expand membrane 4 stretching gain
ok 1 2
this way if you write your favorite pages
2
burn those and save the original 1 save this book
very good
now lower the size and or change the font
does that mean i'll have to be
yes
lighter
i like this better
show 3
this exercise hides codes 2 change 1 mind 4 life
wondered if was seen 4 these words more rhyming
assistance from the other side helps 3 codes of change
intuition flowing within awareness 5 catalyst willing learning
I
catalyst 5 mind

this I knows 4 fun
fun 3 as 2 learning I
learning adjustments yields wisdom assimilation 0 I 2 3 4 5 6
change focus increasing conscious awareness presence YES
ponder nothing 4 length empty 5 attention wise 6 will wake
ME 0 trick remains elusive by confusing subject perception 0
will wonder about wisdom without forcing power WONDER
2 see the things 2 knows without realizing what 2 shows 3
i 3 do know that this I flow 2 assist I goal 2 feel life flow
4 now change chose 3 2 be I thing 3 changing positive
5 initiate dna activation 4 light body 2 ascension
6 i will as such i do
2
i am reading
7
i am what i read
8
law accepted life
9
motion
out of
1141
1142
1122
222
22
11
XI
1151
1111
111111111111111111111111111111111111111111111111

as i 2 start making electronic music
this part is 4 3
thank you
SOUND advice
hear created beat
i VISUALIZE speed
ride the rollercoaster beat
accept rollercoaster as viewpoint camera
allow the scene
LOWs compliment 3
MIDs life core strength source intelligence 4
how HIGH this 1 coaster
flows
how far will this
1
see
3
riding
I
GIVE SPEED as is decreed
FREE
i will 3
0ut c0mes
ME
thank the ride
starts 2 climb
what 1 sees
ride
does
not mind
sharing with
beautiful complexity
exciting the riders or making them wait

it's like a repeating theme that changes shape
still staying
same
it's a harmonic frequency symphony played 4 3
beautiful
life
is 5 experience i hear i learn i write i share
it is 4 you as is 4 me
it is my pleasure
support session concluding
namaste

●